THE COMPUTER PARADE

by Fred D'Ignazio • Illustrations by Stan Gilliam

For Catie and Eric

For Gloria and Carey

Copyright © 1983 by Creative Computing Press.

All rights reserved. No portion of this book may be reproduced — mechanically, electronically, or by any other means, including photocopying — without written permission of the publisher.

Manufactured in the United States of America.

10 9 8 7 6 5 4 3 2 1

ISBN 0-916688-46-1

Library of Congress Number 83-71456

Creative Computing Press
39 E. Hanover Avenue
Morris Plains, New Jersey 07950

Strange noises floated like ghosts into Katie's bedroom. The noises were scary, but Katie was curious.

Katie tiptoed down the stairs and sneaked into the living room. She peeked into the study. Her mother and father were there, leaning over the computer.

Her mother pressed a button, and the computer played music. Katie liked the music. She lay down on a soft rug, feeling warm and dreamy.

Katie awoke. The room was dark and she was alone.

She heard a parade! She ran into the study. Her brother, Eric, was there ahead of her.

Katie and Eric pressed their noses against the glass of the picture screen of the computer, trying to see where the parade music was coming from.

The glass on the picture screen melted

The children tumbled into the computer.

They landed with a loud "SPLASH!" in a railroad car filled with rain water. The Colonel sat on the side, wiggling his toes.

"Hi, Katie! Hi, Eric!" said the Colonel. "Welcome back to Cybernia! What are you kids doing inside the computer?"

"We want to see a parade!" Eric shouted.

"Then follow me," said the Colonel. "You aren't just going to see a parade, you're going to help make one!"

The Colonel put on his shoes and jumped off the railroad car. Katie and Eric chased after him.

They caught up with the Colonel. He was pointing at a long line of people standing beside a railroad track.

"The Parade Bits are from RAM Tower," said the Colonel. "They're here to help you make a parade."

"But how?" Katie asked.

"Climb on this DAC and seesaw up and down," said the Colonel. "Katie, you jump up when you come to a tall Bit. Eric, you jump up when you come to a short Bit."

A duck flew out of the sky and landed on the Colonel's shoulder. "Quack!" said the duck.

"Uh-oh!" the Colonel cried. "Emergency! I've got to go. You kids are on your own. Watch out for Bugs!"

Katie shivered. She remembered the giant spider bug she'd met on her last trip inside the computer. "What kind of bugs?" she asked.

But the Colonel rode away without answering. He couldn't hear her over the loud PUTT! PUTT! PUTT! PUTT! of his motorscooter.

"Don't worry, Katie," said Eric. "If we meet any bugs, I'll squash 'em for you. C'mon, let's make a parade."

Eric jumped up. Katie went down. The DAC began to move. It passed a short Bit. "AAK!" said the Bit.

Next it was Katie's turn. She jumped up and Eric went down. The DAC whizzed by a tall Bit. "EEK!" said the Bit.

The AAKs and EEKs disappeared into a pipe on the side of the DAC.

The DAC moved faster and faster.
Katie looked up. Puffy Volt creatures were floating out of the top of the pipe.

Dozens of Volts mashed together like chains of sticky marshmallows. The chains rippled like waves. The waves turned into dragons. Out of the dragons' mouths marched a parade!

Katie and Eric were so busy watching the parade, they didn't see two Noise Bugs sneak up and hide in the line of Bits. The Bugs switched the children's DAC onto a new track. The new track also had Bits, but they weren't Parade Bits. They were Chemistry Bits.

The Bugs jumped on Eric's head, and he dropped like a stone.
When Eric went down, Katie flew into the air.
Eric closed his eyes. "Help, Katie!" he cried.

Broken, half-formed Volts burst into the sky and smashed together. They turn

to dizzy, mixed-up dragons. The dragons made a parade. But it sounded all wrong.

Katie chased after Eric. She climbed a ladder and swung on a big black lever. The lever switched the DAC back to the track with the Parade Bits. Katie dropped onto the DAC as it zoomed by underneath her.

She shoved the two Noise Bugs off the DAC. "Get out of here!" she yelled. The bugs rolled down a hill into a dirty puddle.

The mixed-up parade vanished. A new parade appeared.

The Colonel galloped up on a camel. "Time to go home!" he said.

"But how?" Katie asked.

"Look up in the sky," said the Colonel.

The children looked. Way up in the sky they saw two dark whirlpools. Dragons flew into the whirlpools and disappeared.

"Those are the Speakers," said the Colonel. "They are your gateway to the world outside the computer."

"How do we get up there?" Eric asked.

"I know how," Katie said. "Let's ride the Volts!" She jumped on a Volt's back and rode it into the sky.

The last Volt flew out of the DAC. With a loud yell, Eric grabbed the creature's tail, then held on tight as the creature dragged him up into the air.

"Good-bye, Katie! Good-bye, Eric!" said the Colonel. "Come back soon!" Then he rode away on his camel.

Katie's Volt became part of one dragon. Eric's Volt became part of another dragon.

The dragons flew toward the Speakers. The children leaned over the side of the dragons and watched Cybernia and the computer parade get smaller and smaller.

The dragons dived into the whirlpools.
"Hold on!" Katie cried.

The dragons turned into lightnir

ith sharp, jagged teeth.

"Katie! Eric! Wake up!"

Katie opened her eyes.

"Time for breakfast!" her mother called.

Katie rolled over and nudged Eric. "We're home," she whispered.

"We are?" Eric said. He kissed the rug and held it tight.

Their mother entered the room. "What are you children doing in here?" she asked.

"We made a parade inside the computer," said Katie.

"And we're going back right after breakfast!" said Eric.

About the Author and Illustrator

FRED D'IGNAZIO is a freelance writer currently living in Roanoke, Virginia, with his wife, Janet, his two children, Catie and Eric, and his cat Mow-Mow. Fred has written numerous children's books about computers, including *Katie and the Computer* (with Stan Gilliam, Creative Computing Press, 1979), *The Star Wars Question & Answer Book About Computers,* and *Chip Mitchell: The Case of the Stolen Computer Brains.*

STAN GILLIAM is a freelance designer and illustrator currently living in Chapel Hill, North Carolina. He has a master's degree in Educational Media Design and has worked on several projects for children. These include *Katie and the Computer* and interactive exhibits for the North Carolina Museum of Life and Science. He is also a painter who exhibits his work frequently, and a former college art instructor.

Pictorial Flowchart of the Computer Parade

Katie and Eric Hear Parade Music
Katie and Eric's mother has written a Parade Program on the family computer. When the program runs, it changes electronic pulses into sounds that resemble parade music.

The Children Fall into the Computer
The way into the computer is through the computer TV screen "window." The children's fall represents their journey into the tiny microchip world of the computer.

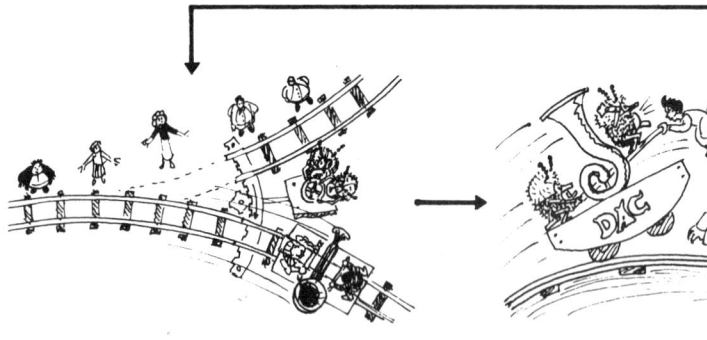

The Noise Bugs Derail the DAC
The Noise Bugs hide among the Parade Bits. They are a mistake in the Parade Program. They make the DAC jump to an unexpected new location in the computer memory. The new section of memory stores a Chemistry Program written by Katie's mother.

The DAC is Out of Control
The Chemistry Bits make the DAC loop around in circles to process certain bits several times. The cave represents the edge of memory. If the DAC journeys past the outer bounds of memory, without the Colonel's supervision, it will "crash," and the computer will stop working.

The Mixed-Up Parade
The DAC tries to process the Chemistry Bits as if they were Parade Bits. The Chemistry Bits produce voltage waves that represent random sounds — i.e., noise.

Katie Rescues Eric
Katie guides the DAC back to the section of memory that stores the remaining Parade Bits. When the DAC converts these bits it makes voltage waves that will generate parade music again.